onward &
upward

sayings to insprire and motivate

Tom Burns

to: ....

on the occasion of: ....

....

date: ....

from: ....

axis ● books

First published in the UK by Axis Books Ltd
© 2012 Axis Books Limited

All rights reserved. No part of this book may
be reproduced in any form,by photostat,
microfilm, xerography, or any other means, or
incorporated into any information retrieval
system, electronic or mechanical, without the
written permission of the copyright owner.

Printed and bound in China
9 8 7 6 5 4 3 2 1

Conceived and created by
Axis Books Limited,
8c Accommodation Road,
London NW11 8ED

www.axisbooks.co.uk

Creative Director: Siân Keogh
Designer: Marie Christou
Production: Bili Books

ISBN 978-1-908621-17-7

about this book

Onward & Upward is an inspirational collection of phrases and sayings on the value of trying as a means of success. It is guaranteed to motivate anyone whose personal or professional life needs a boost. These words of wisdom, compiled from the thoughts of people from around the world and all walks of life, show that success comes from trying, keeping a positive attitude, relishing a challenge and refusing to be led off track by a setback. These words will demonstrate that whatever has happened in the past, in the present and future you will succeed.

Complemented by a beautiful collection of gently amusing animal photographs, these thoughts and sayings are sure to motivate anyone to succeed, whatever their goal.

You can have a
fresh start any
moment you choose.

Be confident of

your ability…

…and tough enough

to follow through.

To win a battle,

you may need to fight

it more than once.

Character is doing
the right thing when
nobody's looking.

Life is an opportunity.

Well done is
better than
well said.

You must remain

focused on your

journey to greatness.

Nothing is

standing in

your way.

If you don't start
today, you won't
finish tomorrow.

Fill your heart with good
things, and good things
will come your way.

An optimist sees
the opportunity in
every difficulty.

Scaling the mountain is
what makes the view from
the top so wonderful.

The heaviest burdens are placed on those with the shoulders to carry them.

I can is 100 times more important than IQ.

Success is a

state of mind.

Many of the great achievements

of the world were accomplished

by tired and discouraged men

who kept on working.

Do not lose courage.

"Not now" fast

becomes "never."

Worrying about yesterday's failures means today's successes will be few and far between.

Everyone who got

where he is had to

begin where he was.

The more you want to

get something done,

the less likely you

are to call it work.

If you think you can…

…you can.

Things never go so
well that you should
have no fear, and never
so badly that you
should have no hope.

You can't leave where
you are until you decide
where you want to be.

Making money is easy, making a difference is not.

Work is the
price of success.

Anyone who wastes

one hour of life

does not understand

the value of life.

Much effort,

much prosperity.

Don't follow the crowd:

that's the easiest

way to get lost.

You don't have to
be great to start…

…but you have to
start to be great.

The goal and the

price are the

same: life itself.

To guarantee success,

act as if it were

impossible to fail.

Advance confidently
in the direction of
your dreams, and you'll
meet with success.

It takes courage to
turn out to be who
you really are.

Bad habits are like
a comfortable bed,
easy to get into but
hard to get out of.

Laughing at your weaknesses makes you strong.

The only limitation

is in your own mind.

The miracle is not to
fly in the air, or to
walk on the water, but
to walk on the earth.

Dare not to be something…

…dare to be someone.

Greatness is not in where we stand, but in which direction we are moving.

Believe in something

and it will happen.

Obstacles are stepping
stones in disguise.

What counts is not the number of hours you put in, but how much you put in the hours.

Nobody got anywhere
in the world by
simply being content.

Enthusiasm is

faith set on fire.

If you think you'll
lose, you're lost.

Success is failure
turned inside out.

The more you sweat,

the luckier you get.

The way to succeed
is never to quit.

Unless you are ambitious,
you do not make progress.

When the going gets tough,
winners hang in until the
going gets easier.

Talk is cheap because
supply exceeds demand.

The best success

is built on failure.

A lost opportunity

never comes back.

The only limits

are those of vision.

Winners never quit
and quitters never win.

The shortest

answer is doing.

Success is laughing

often and much.

If you can't modify
your dreams, magnify
your skills.

Whatever you do, do it heartily.

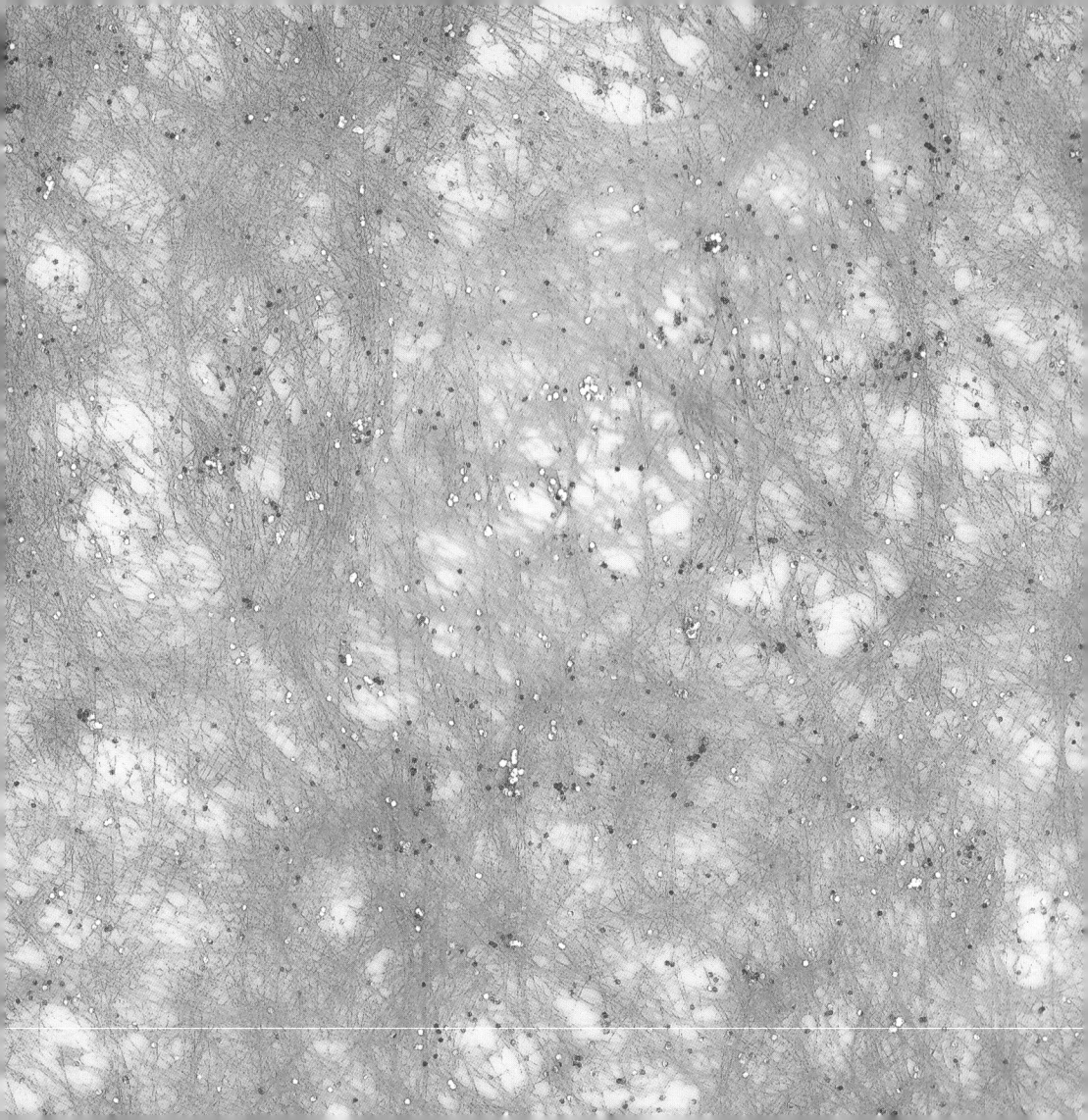